THE ART OF BEING
HUMAN

"It's great to find an accessible book that says something quite profound about the human condition.
This wasn't my opinion half way through the book. I struggled with how sacred spiritual beliefs were being compared to things like football and shopping. By the end the book, though, its wisdom and humaneness drew me in, expanding my awareness of my attitudes towards other people's beliefs and giving me insight into a possible explanation for some of the conflicts I have experienced over the years."

A Seeker

"A revealing window into the mind and its workings, making sense of our behaviour and giving many handles by which to grab hold of that slippery thing, life. Hayes has one of those rare writing styles, where the writing itself contains a significant part of the meaning."

An Intellect

"This is a daringly honest mirror-of-a-book. Hayes' clever prose, wit and wisdom makes looking into it not only an entertaining and edifying experience, but also an extremely important one for all who champion peace, compassion and love."

A Romantic

"*The Art of Being Human* invites you to look at yourself and also step into the shoes of others and see the world through their eyes. Yet reading this book is only half the story - the real issue is how much you dwell on the questions it poses."

A Journalist

Quote on front cover by Paul Davies

THE ART OF BEING
HUMAN

JOHN HAYES

VISIONSHIP

First published in Great Britain in 2010 by Visionship Books
This revised edition published in 2011 by Visionship Books

Copyright @ 2010 by John Hayes

The moral right to the author has been asserted

All rights reserved
No part of this publication may be reproduced, stored in a retrieval system, or transmitted in any form or by any means, without the prior written permission of the publisher, nor be otherwise circulated in any form of binding or cover other than that in which it is published and without a similar condition being imposed on the subsequent purchaser

A CIP catalogue record for this book is available from the British Library

Paperback ISBN: 978-0-9558071-1-4
eBook Adobe Digital Editions ISBN: 978-0-9558071-2-1
eBook Mobipocket ISBN: 978-0-9558071-3-8
eBook Adobe Reader format ISBN: 978-0-9558071-4-5

Cover design by Visionship Books

Printed in England by
CPI Antony Rowe, Wiltshire

Visionship Books

www.visionship.co.uk

To Annabel and Michael

Contents

	A Therapist's View	1
1	Special Ones	13
2	Members	19
3	Brands	23
4	Believers	26
5	Spiritualists	29
6	Players	33
7	Artists	37
8	Romantics	40
9	Time Travellers	45
10	Reflections	50
11	Biological Immortals	54
12	Trippers	58
13	Procrastinators	61
14	Threesomes	66
15	Know-it-alls	69
16	Happy Enders	73
	A Therapist's View II	77
	A Personal View	93

A Therapist's View

If you are like me, when you pick up a book with the subtitle, *A Therapist's View of Romance, Football, Evolution & Heaven*, a part of you is curious to explore questions that the rest of you either shrugs off as irrelevant or spends an awful lot of time trying to avoid.

Questions like, *Why do I believe in love? Why do I sleep around? Why do I fanatically support a football team? Why do I spend a fortune on brand-name items? Why do I believe in God? Why don't I believe in God?*

If you already have answers to these questions, I am not about to challenge them. Nor do I possess a psychological reality, spiritual truth or scientific fact with which to enlighten you.

What I offer with this book is a perspective on life that allows you to more meaningfully empathise and connect with people whose beliefs and behaviour conflict with your own. It is the view that, regardless of whether you see the world through the eyes of a romantic, football fanatic, spiritualist or atheist, you are haunted and inspired by the same skeleton in the cupboard as everyone else.

To reveal the identity of this ghoulish secret, we must draw on the same curious part of us that on dark, stormy nights, compelled us as children to crawl from under the bed covers towards the mysterious knocking sound coming from inside the wardrobe, as opposed to the part wanting to remain motionless under the covers in the hope that whatever lurked in the darkness would somehow overlook us and go away.

Of course, you and I are not children any more. The things we are drawn towards, or hide from, no longer inhabit wardrobes. They exist in the real world as people with names and faces, as diseases that spread and accidents waiting to happen.

The particular degree to which you fear certain people and situations is coloured by your experiences that lurk as memories in your mind and which, when triggered, spill out into the present, warping and distorting it into a nightmare that is often a struggle to awaken from.

A Therapist's View

That I, the author of this book, am a hypnotherapist may have you expecting to be led through a secret door to this shadowy world within and, armed with a metaphorical sword and flower, help you slay or befriend your fear and free some innocent core self.

Such a door to the past certainly exists, but it is not one we will be opening together. Rather, we will be tiptoeing around a door that exists in your future.

If I were writing a fairy tale for children, this door would be encrusted with diamonds and, etched in gold above an emerald knocker, would be the enigma, *Open this door and you will never return. Ignore it and you will never have really been here.* The door, like certain stars, could only be glimpsed by looking away from it, just long enough for the child-hero in the fable to recognise the door as something infinite and to embark on a quest to rediscover it.

This is an adult book, though, and if you are like most grown-ups the door is embedded so deeply in your unconscious that you rarely get to perceive its presence. This is probably quite a good thing because, were the door really to bob to the surface of your awareness, it would drive you mad in the same way that a skeleton emerging from a cupboard would on a dark, stormy night.

I am referring, of course, to the portal that exists because of the fragile and finite nature of your existence. The door to the great beyond. The proverbial bucket we all kick. The black hole in our awareness. The secret trapdoor.

Death's door.

We all know we are going to die. We just do not know how, where or when, exactly. You probably assume, like everyone else, that it will be sometime other than *now* which, if a meteor travelling at a typical meteoric speed is on a collision course with Earth, will be before you reach the end of this page. In fact, while reading this very sentence, one of your genes may be sending the first suicidal instruction for a cell to embark on a mission to seek and destroy, aka the Big C. Or the instant you picked up this book, an unstoppable chain of events leading to your accidental demise may have been set in motion. And if traumas, faulty genes, predators and chance do not kill you, old age will gradually creep up and nudge you through death's door. Whether you are happy or sad, young or old, healthy or ill, you are *terminally human*.

We are all terminally human

A Therapist's View

For some people, being *terminally human* fills them with dread. The shadow of death seems to be everywhere and in everything. It reaches out through the encroaching branches of a neighbour's tree. It oozes out as mistrust of salesmen knocking at the door. It reverberates in the chilling regret, *Life has passed me by and I missed it.* Death surfaces every night in their dreams, chasing them through labyrinths and bobbing to the surface of eerily still oceans.

In my profession as a therapist, we refer to this dread of death as *death anxiety* or *existential angst*. I have witnessed it erupt through the surface only once. It happened to an extremely brave and terminally ill friend of mine for whom exhaustion momentarily stripped her of her usually robust defences, revealing a truly frightened, vicious and childlike self. It was a harrowing experience for both of us.

This book is not, though, for the terrified few. It is for the rest of us, yourself included perhaps, who manage to keep death anxiety at bay. So much so that most of the time we hardly notice it at all, except for a few blips during adolescence and the mid-life crisis.

Most of us manage to keep death anxiety at bay so well that we hardly notice it at all

Regardless of how strong our defences or how healthy we are, anxiety still seeps into our lives and into our dreams. It happens when we feel unsafe, vulnerable and out of control. And it is not just the big things like neglect, abuse, trauma and loss that make our hearts beat faster, stomachs churn and hands tremble. It is also the little, everyday things like when we make the first move on a date, not knowing if we will be accepted or rejected, or perhaps completely humiliated. It happens during an interview or at a party when prospective employees and friends scrutinise and judge us. It occurs when our football team gives away a last-minute penalty and we know that if the opposing team scores, we lose and will be eliminated from the competition.

You may not immediately associate your own anxiety with a fear of dying, but all anxiety is the experience of feeling unsafe because our physical, emotional and spiritual identities are threatened. And death is the ultimate identity destroyer. It is everyone's most primordial fear and one that cannot be banished. The best we can do is to acknowledge our fear, reflect on it and embrace it as best we can in a way that enables us to live in harmony with ourselves, other people and the world we inhabit.

A Therapist's View

All anxiety is the experience of our identities being threatened. And death is the ultimate identity destroyer

Now I do not know any more about death than the next person because I have never died. But I have felt unsafe, vulnerable and out of control. I have loved and lost. And I know an awful lot about how to avoid feeling unsafe and afraid. I am a master of evasion. An expert in the art of illusion.

If you are like me and endeavour to keep your fear of death at a safe distance, your first line of defence is to convince yourself that you are not afraid. You laugh at death using little Woody Allen-like quips such as, *It's not that I am afraid of dying. I just don't want to be there when it happens!* You philosophise about death by humbly pointing out that you *have had a good innings.* You are pragmatic about your death, reminding people matter-of-factly that, *We live, we die. That's life. We all have to go sometime.* If you possess a strong teenage spirit you may even taunt death by going bungee jumping, driving at a hundred miles per hour or going on mad fairground rides.

Our first line of defence against death is to convince ourselves that we are not afraid

Regardless of what you boast down the pub or over a coffee, like everyone, you will have adopted and developed extremely complex beliefs, alliances and ways of behaving that help keep your existential angst from piercing the surface. These may include the belief that an alternative destiny awaits you, that your God will save you or that a medical advance will cure you. You may fight those who threaten you, woo those who can protect you, invest in products that keep you looking young or take drugs that keep you anxiety free.

Your own particular beliefs, alliances and behaviour are what separates you from, and connects you with, other people. They make you uniquely *you*.

Being such a complex, multifaceted human individual, you probably have a myriad of often conflicting beliefs and ways of behaving, each combination of which constitutes a different way of being you - referred to in this book as your *identities*.

How do the beliefs, alliances and ways of behaving that make up your multiple *identities* shield you against your fear of death? They provide you with the *essentials of being* that you require to feel confident, safe and alive. These include a sense of permanence, feeling you are special, feeling you belong, feeling in control of your life, physical intimacy, meaning, purpose and hope.

> *Our identities provide us with the essentials of being that we need to feel vibrantly connected to life*

Before we embark on a tour of the *identities* you, yourself may have developed to provide you with your own *essentials of being*, I would like to make it absolutely clear that by referring to them as *identities*, I am not suggesting they exist as autonomous selves. They are simply *ways of being* that help reduce existential angst and which, by naming, defining and owning can provide you with an alternative way to view yourself and others.

I am not putting into question whether your own *identities* are good or bad, right or wrong, true or not true. Nor am I siding with agnostics, hedonists, atheists, spiritualists or believers. I am simply offering an empathic, humane and inclusive perspective on the beliefs, alliances and behaviour that traditionally separate and divide us - the Gods we pray to, the football teams we support and the science we use to explain ourselves.

Will you struggle or sail through this book?

Inspired by your own way of seeing the world, your feelings towards my portrayal of the sixteen *identities* that populate this book will, at different points along the way, have you struggling or compelled to turn the pages.

There may well be passages during which you effortlessly go with the flow, as if the book were a kindred spirit putting into words what you already know.

Other passages may prompt the kind of smile of recognition that curls your lips when someone alludes to a side of your character you know to be true, but which you are not always ready to admit.

Or you may find yourself unmoved by the matter-of-fact treatment of *identities* you barely recognise, and to keep the pages turning, you flit between *identities*, lingering on those that intrigue and amuse you, and skimming over those that alienate and bemuse you.

You may grow irritated by what you consider to be the superficial treatment of those *identities* that, for you and billions of others, embody deeply held and sacred beliefs. You may even feel personally affronted that football and shopping are given equal recognition as providers of meaning and purpose to world religions and love. Sometimes, though, to appreciate the worth of another's source of solace and joy, it is necessary to distance ourselves from our own; just as to glimpse the stars in the sky above, we must allow our own star to sink below the horizon. So, if you do find yourself struggling to appreciate the value of some *identities*, imagine, while reading the book, that you are gazing up at the firmament on a moon-less night, pondering the private life of someone else's sun.

Of course, it may not be just mild irritation that hampers your flow. A part of you may feel so enraged by the book's reluctance to adequately appreciate your own "truth" that you are momentarily tempted to sever your relationship with the book. In such moments, unlikely as it may seem, the last two chapters may surprise you, in the same way that a peek into the heart of an old foe might surprise you. Instead of trivialising your world view, the conclusion may enrich and enhance it with a perspective that enables you to more meaningfully empathise and connect with people who see the world through very different eyes.

That is the aim of this book. To provide a glimpse of how, no matter what we believe, whom we ally ourselves with or how we behave, we are all united by our struggle to keep at bay the same existential angst that is an inescapable part of being terminally human.

So, with all these possibilities embedded somewhere along the way, let us begin. The first of the *identities* that may be helping you keep your own existential angst at bay is the belief that you are somehow different from everyone else. That you are *special*.

1

Special Ones

Do you believe you are here for a special purpose?

To be a *special one* you do not have to know why you are special. You simply feel it inside. You intuit that a unique destiny awaits you, or sense that you are on a mission of some kind. Embedded in your unconscious lies a secret you have glimpsed and are trying to remember.

Once, as children, we were all *special ones*. We communicated with invisible friends, believed in fairies and identified with immortal superheroes like Superman, Batman, Wonder Woman and She-Rah.

As children we were all special ones

Then we grew up. We learned about the laws of

nature and how they had to be obeyed. We identified with characters that were more human, their missions more plausible and sophisticated. Characters like Neo from the film *The Matrix*.

Neo is a *special one* because he chooses to change the story that destiny has written for him - that of a frustrated computer programmer by day and an illegal hacker by night.

Neo's *special* story begins late one night when someone hacks into his computer and instructs him to *follow the white rabbit.* The message means nothing to Neo until, almost simultaneously, he receives a knock on the door from a group of partygoers, one of whom has a white rabbit tattooed on her shoulder.

The unlikely coincidence prompts Neo to *follow the white rabbit* to a man called Morpheus who reveals to him the following "truth": The life Neo has been leading is not real. It is a computer-generated simulation of reality called the *Matrix* created by intelligent, self-replicating machines to keep Neo's mind alive while his comatose body charges the giant generators the machines need to function.

Deep within the bowels of this post-apocalyptic *real* world ruled by the machines, a community of humans have managed to escape being plugged into the

Matrix. Morpheus is one of the few who believe that Neo is the prophesied *One* who can free the rest of humanity from their illusory existence. For Neo to fulfil the prophecy, he must choose between one of two pills. If he chooses one pill, he wakes up in the computer-generated life he believed to be real and forgets everything he has learned about the *Matrix*. If he takes the other, he is unplugged from his illusory existence and trained to use his mind to bend the rules of the *Matrix* so that when he is plugged back in, he is able to dodge bullets, fly, and even resurrect himself when he dies.

For many adolescent *special ones*, Neo's "truth" appeals to our rampant imaginations. Those of us who have matured connect with a world that is far more subtle, enigmatic and poetic. The stories we relate to are allegories and fables that hint at life's mysterious "truth", like *The Alchemist* by Paulo Coelho.

The protagonist of *The Alchemist* is a poor shepherd boy called Santiago who has always desired to travel. One afternoon, while taking a siesta in the ruin of an abandoned church, Santiago dreams of a treasure buried near the pyramids of Egypt. The next day Santiago has the same dream and, in his search for an interpretation, he chances upon an old man who bestows on him the following wisdom: "Whoever you are, and whatever you do, when you really want something, it is because the desire was born in the soul of the universe. It is your mission on Earth."

In other words, Santiago has a desire to travel because his journey is already embedded in the universe. All Santiago has to do to realise his dream and unearth the treasure is to follow his own footprints that manifest themselves in dreams, as coincidences, signs and déjà vu experiences.

The essence of Santiago's story is not that different from that of Neo's. For both to realise their special destiny, they must relinquish the security their old life afforded them. Neo must forego the comforts of a digital dream world. Santiago must give up his flock of sheep and his identity as a shepherd. Both connect with a twin world. Neo's is a post-apocalyptic real world dominated by machines. Santiago's is the "true" life he glimpses in his dreams. Both have a wise helper. Neo's is the faithful warrior Morpheus. Santiago's is a king with powers of foresight who represents Santiago's own inspiration. Both have a mission. Neo's is to save humanity. Santiago's is to discover his true self, represented in the story by the buried treasure.

Special Ones

If you are a *special one*, the stories of Neo and Santiago may or may not resonate with you. Like them, though, you have experienced a flash of inspiration or had a great idea. You allow your instincts and intuition to override logic and reason. You give meaning to signs and coincidences. You have had glimpses of clarity when you have seen beyond the limitations you have imposed upon yourself.

For most *special ones*, these experiences were most prolific in our youth. The world was our oyster. Anything seemed possible. We swaggered along, flaunting our invincibility. Even the most haunted, unhappy among us could cut and starve ourselves in the belief that we were somehow immune to death.

The child psychologist, David Elkind, has this to say about the invincibility of youth and their belief in a special destiny: "The belief in their own uniqueness and specialness, in their own personal fable, leads to the concept that the laws of nature do not apply to them. Teenagers believe that nothing bad will happen to them, that they will not suffer the consequences of their actions because it is not part of their fable."

As a *special one*, you too have a burning, adolescent spirit, only rather than proudly holding aloft your own torch, you allow yourself to be guided by a twinkling inner star that remains forever invisible to the casual observer.

Your specialness is not something you readily discuss or admit to. It is a private, silent belief.

As a *special one* you have no need to fear death because the laws of nature that apply to everybody else, like death and dying, do not apply to you. You are master of your own alternative destiny.

Essentials of Being
Specialness, meaning and purpose.

2

Members

Do you strongly identify with a team, nation, class or ideology?

If you are a *member*, other *members* may not immediately recognise you but once you identify yourself, if your identity matches you instantly connect, regardless of whether you have met before or like one another. That which unites you is the history and goals of the *group* to which you both belong.

The primal and most natural *group* to which all *members* belong is the family. Like all groups it has the potential to exist forever. Family *members* may die and be substituted by other *members*, but the family genes remain imperishable. They are immortal. The fact that you are reading this book means that your own family is already millions of years old.

The most primal immortal group we belong to is our family

Sadly, relationships between family *members* sometimes break down or tragedy separates us. Isolated *members* search for substitute groups that provide us with the belonging we yearn for. We join clubs, unions, circles, cults, leagues and brotherhoods.

For many men, and increasingly more women, one of the most common substitute groups is the football club. In the same way that *members* of a family are relatives, supporters of the same team are kindred spirits. We wear the same colours, bask in the same reflected glory and bathe in the same vicarious success. We seek one another out to gain safety in numbers. At matches, we chant as if a single voice. We cheer and boo at the same time for the same reasons. We experience the same communal ecstasy when our team scores and the same despair when our team concedes. After a near miss we all go *Oooooooh* and hold our head in our hands.

Sometimes, so strong is our attachment to our team that we talk as if we *are* our team. We boast about how *we* scored, how *we* won, how brilliant *we* were. How *we* are the best. As one of football's most famous authors, Nick Hornby, said of himself when his team won the league and cup double, "As far as I was concerned I *was* Arsenal and entitled to my triumphant bliss."

For others who are at a loss to understand a football supporter's fanaticism, Hornby explains: "We do not lack imagination, nor have we had sad and barren lives; it is just that real life is paler, duller and contains less potential for unexpected delirium."

There are other benefits that come from supporting a football team. Watching our team play, whether in a stadium, a pub or alone at home, provides us with a way to express emotions that we may otherwise suppress. Feelings such as passion, sadness and delirium. Group hysteria serves as a catalyst for these emotions. Football helps us feel alive.

What does supporting a team have to do with our fear of death? Well, football clubs are like families. They, too, have the potential to live forever. Each team's fortunes may vary, but they provide those of us who belong and who *are* our team, with an immortal identity. Here is the official identity of one well-known football club, referred to here as *your team*. Even if you do not support a team, remove the football references and you may recognise it as your own.

"*Your team* is an institution in world football, that combines the traditions of an illustrious past with a visionary outlook for the future. *Your* way is one of dignity, honesty and respect, offering a sense of belonging and a quiet confidence in the future. There is no disgrace in striving for success, but it has to be done in the right way, within the spirit of the game."

This kind of immortal identity is not just provided by football clubs. Political parties, ideologies, circles and sects all have their own mottos and dicta that provide their *members* with an immortal status.

If you are a *member* and one of *us*, you and I may die, but *we*, the group, live on forever.

Essentials of Being
Belonging.

3

Brands

Are you a shopaholic prepared to spend a small fortune on brand-name items?

If you are a *brand* you are easy to spot. Your identity is emblazoned across your chest, embroidered onto your clothes, glued to your handbags and soldered onto the bonnets of your cars. You are a walking advert. And why not advertise yourself? You are a denizen of the human race. One of the desirables. You are what everyone else wants to be.

Your own identifying mark may be nothing more than a splash of colour, a stylised initial or a logo. So recognisable and evocative, however, is your mark that just a glimpse of it by a passer-by is enough to communicate to them everything they need to know about you. Not consciously perhaps, but certainly at a subliminal level. Here is what one of your identifying marks may be saying about you.

You are a competitor in the game of life. An athlete in every sense of the word. You are determined and accomplished, yet still you strive to exceed yourself and are not afraid to break the mould to do so. You are no ordinary human being. You are an icon for action and excellence. You are free and independent. Whatever obstacles are put in your way, you will overcome them. Social restraints and physical impediments mean nothing to you. Others talk and dream about how to live life. You *just do it*.

Bingo! You are *Nike*.

How about this one? Just a whiff of you and others know you are the embodiment of sophistication, romance, sexiness, glamour and beauty. You are abstract and unique. You are cool, confident and unflappable. You are Paris on a breezy autumn day. You are a lover, kissing on the banks of the Seine. You are Nicole Kidman dressed as Marilyn Monroe with a thousand paparazzi swooning at your feet. You are Kate Moss. You are Keira Knightley. You are *Chanel*.

What does being a *brand* have to do with keeping death anxiety at bay? Quite a lot. The products we associate with are timeless symbols of perfection that embody success, desirability and power.

Brands are desirable, powerful and eternal

By "branding" ourselves, we become, by association, everything the brand stands for – power, beauty and perfection. Brands elevate our self-esteem and give us an immortal identity in the same way that successful groups do for their *members.*

Companies that create brands are well aware of the impact brands have on our core anxiety levels. Here is a quote from the *Journal of Consumer Research*: "Consumers with anxiety about their existence are especially in need of the symbolic security that brand connection provides. Materialistic individuals form strong connections to their brand when death anxiety is high but not when death anxiety is low."

Of course, we *brands* are well aware of the tricks of advertisers, but our unconscious mind that receives their suggestions falls for them every time.

As a *brand*, you are a timeless archetype of beauty, power and perfection. An image than cannot die.

Essentials of being
Specialness.

4

Believers

Do you believe that death is a door to another life?

Those of us who believe in life after death do not simply amble up to death's door, tug at the bell chord and expect to be invited into a pool of light, or receive a pat on the back before being whisked back to earth in another body. We believe that our progression into the next life is determined by our moral conduct in this life, judged either by an omnipotent creator or the indifference of karma.

To ensure that our next life is better than our last is no mean feat. We must purify our hearts, purge our minds and free our immaculate souls. This requires a considerable amount of self-control, sacrifice, meditation and prayer, not to mention a huge leap of faith. After all, everything we do, think and feel is taken into account. We can be no-one other than ourselves.

Our progression into the next life is determined by our moral actions in this one

For those of us who are judged worthy, there are many names and ways of understanding the place that awaits us the other side of death's door. Muslims among us have the delights of Jannah to look forward to. Christian readers will ascend to a glorious Heaven. Orthodox Jews will resurrect in the Messianic age with the coming of the Messiah. Jehovah's Witnesses will resurrect in the flesh in an Edenic Earth. Christian Scientists will attain a new bodiless level of consciousness. Mormons among us will undergo instruction, preparation and judgement in the Spirit World before our spirit and body reunite forever through resurrection. The soul of Wiccans will rest and reflect in Summerland before reincarnating into another life. The souls of Hindus and other holders of the Universal Truth will transmigrate time and again in a process called samsara until our individual self realises its unity with our universal self and we become one with God through salvation. Sikhs among us participate in a similar cycle of transmigration in order that we can overcome our ego and free ourselves from the cycle to experience salvation in *Sach khand*, the realm of Truth where the soul exists eternally as an entity of radiant light. Buddhists among us also reincarnate but we have no soul. Our transmigration we liken to successive candles that burn with the same flame until, finally, the candle extinguishes itself and we are liberated from the cycle of life and death, entering instead the non-dualistic, incomprehensible and unutterable *Nirvana*.

To others it may seem that we *believers* are divided by our different faiths, sects, schisms and divisions, but we are all bound by one belief: after death comes life.

As a *believer*, you have no need to fear death because death is a door to another life.

Essentials of Being
Permanence, belonging, meaning, purpose and hope.

5

Spiritualists

Do you have a cosmic, multidimensional self?

We *spiritualists* do not have to die to discover what lies beyond death's door. We who believe that dream logic is as real as evidence-based logic have other doors – portals in the mind through which information can be channelled and through which our multidimensional selves can travel.

Guided by our intuition, we venture beyond the five-sensory world of our biological being and reconnect with our cosmic self. We are warriors of love in a universe in which everything is the vibrating energy of condensed light. Sound, colour, emotions, you and I are all its frequencies.

Our mission in this life is to heal ourselves and those around us by raising the frequency of love. To accomplish our mission we use tarot, astrology and runes to tap into the wisdom of the universe. We employ crystals, symbols and sound to align our chakras. We dance and chant to awaken our Kundalini. We use psychic surgery to patch up karmic wounds. We employ pendulums to identify the holes in our auras. We enter trance to heal traumas in our past lives. We accompany our shamanic power animals in search of answers from ancestors and angles that inhabit the spirit world.

We *spiritualists* awaken in the dream others call life and use our intention to reveal reality. We transcend the limits of our three-dimensional world and embrace our multidimensional cosmic origins. We re-become who we really are.

Spiritualists remember who we really are

If you have sensed the muffled calling of your multidimensional self, one group of cosmic ancestors that may have come knocking on your door are the Pleiadian Light Beings. They are a collective of extraterrestrials that hail from the Pleiadian Star System, traversing space and time to help you reveal your celestial heritage and restore Earth and the human version of life to the forefront of creation. Here is what one Pleiadian communicated through an interpreter and conduit of the spirit named Barbara Marciniak. "We ask you to re-evaluate the purpose of your life, to redefine the forces that rule you, to resurrect the codes of consciousness stored in your being. It is time for you to reclaim your knowledge as a creator through thought, to recall the purpose of the Living Library of Earth, to restore beauty through value of life, and to remember who you are."

Another cosmic entity that may be trying to contact you is the thetan. The name might not ring a bell, but you may have heard of Scientology. If not, you have almost certainly heard of Tom Cruise, John Travolta, Kirstie Alley or Lisa Presley. All of them are Scientologists. Tom Cruise even has his own church.

According to Scientology mythology, thetans are the true identity of a person. Your own thetan self is your intrinsically good, omniscient, nonmaterial core, capable of unlimited energy. Thetans brought the material universe into being but fell from grace when they began to identify with their creations, rather than with their original state of purity, eventually losing their memory of their true nature, along with their associated spiritual and creative powers. Your mission as a human being is to remember your thetan origin and regain your divine powers. Fortunately, thetans are reborn time and again through a process called assumption, so you will have plenty of opportunities.

As a *spiritualist* yourself, you may have had little or no contact with Pleiadian Light Beings, thetans or any other recognisable cosmic entity for that matter. In fact, like the majority of *spiritualists*, you probably have little interest in cosmic mythologies and missions to save the planet. You simply look beyond the physical world and use your intention to synchronise with your true self because, as the psychologist and Reiki Master Paula Horan put it, "Given the fragility of the human body, security in the physical world does not exist. For this reason, it is a waste of time dedicating hours of your precious life feeding the illusion that security exists. Only by trusting in your True Self, not subject to physical death, will you gain peace within."

As a *spiritualist*, you have no need to fear death because your *other you* is immortal.

Essentials of being
Specialness, control, meaning, purpose and hope.

6

Players

Are you predatory, seductive or competitive?

If you are a *player*, you compete in the Game of Life and have a single goal: to win.

Winning the Game of Life can mean different things for different *players*. It can mean marrying the person you love, getting the pay rise you deserve, reaching the summit of the mountain you prize, holding aloft the trophy you covet or crossing the finishing line first.

Whatever winning means, we *players* have a vast array of tools, skills and resources to help us succeed. If it is love we seek, we have roses, chocolates, candlelight and poetry. If it is sex we desire, we have lipstick, Wonderbras, money and fast cars. If we want to climb to the top of a mountain, we have ropes, backpacks and super-light fleeces.

Being a *player* is not all fun and games. Dedicated *players* are focused, disciplined and determined. We train hard, and play hard. Our sinews and nerves are always primed, our adrenalin always pumping, our eyes glued to our goal. So immersed are we in the Game of Life that there is no time to reflect on who made the rules and why.

Only a few historians of the game reflect on the game's purpose. Evolutionary biologists among us believe that there is only one purpose: to reproduce with a desirable mate so as to ensure not only our own survival, but the survival of our species. In other words, we are simply biological entities whose destiny it is to be born, procreate and then die as natural selection plays out the possibly meaningless game of evolution.

At different periods in the game's history, the winners in this Game of Life – the most potent, desirable and resourceful – have found different ways to successfully sire and rear offspring. Nowadays, we tend to engage in long-term, monogamous relationships to ensure that our children are our own. In the past (and quite possibly in the future), engaging in multiple relationships was equally successful. Mothers knew their young would be protected by every male because they were all potential fathers. For males, it increased their chances of fathering more children.

Whether we are monogamous or polygamous, use cunning, brute force, charm, seduction or the promise of a secure home to ensure we secure a mate, nature has developed a way of ensuring our participation: the fleeting moment of bliss that comes with the act of copulation - the orgasm.

We are biological entities whose destiny it is to be born, procreate and then die as natural selection plays out the possibly meaningless game of evolution

Some evolutionists take this view of the Game of Life a step further by relegating human *players* to the rank of mere pawns in another more ancient version of the Game; the version in which the true *players* are strands of unemotional, inanimate DNA. In this more primordial game, we humans, along with all other living creatures, are merely hosts that DNA uses to replicate itself. As the evolutionary biologist Richard Dawkins put it in *The Selfish Gene*, "Individuals are not stable things, they are fleeting. Chromosomes, too, are shuffled to oblivion, like hands of cards soon after they are dealt. But the cards themselves survive the shuffling. The cards are the genes. The genes are not destroyed by crossing-over, they merely change partners and march on. They are the replicators and we are their survival machines. When we have served our purpose we are cast aside. But genes are the denizens of geological time. Genes are forever."

Whether we humans are major *players* in the Game of Life or just the improbable hosts to a string of unemotional DNA that use us as survival machines, the premise of the Game of Life remains the same - to go on existing.

As a *player*, death may be something you fear, but all the while you feel pleasured, desired and potent, you are a long way away from that fear.

Essential of Being
Control, power and physical intimacy.

7

Artists

Do you write, sculpture, paint or compose?

To be an *artist,* you do not have to be gifted, just expressive and creative.

In a sense, we are all *artists*. Just by getting up in the morning, we are expressing a thought and creating change. We leave behind an unmade bed, meticulously folded sheets or an indent in the pillow. We create a trail of footprints that proves we exist.

Such artwork, though, is not the work of true *artists*. Such trails are like footprints in the sand. They have no distinguishing marks and get washed away with the passing of time, leaving no trace. The bed could have been made or left unmade by anyone. The indent in the pillow could have been made by any head.

What distinguishes true *artists* is that we inhabit our

creations. When someone stumbles upon one of our self-expressions, they know we are the author. Our artwork is a self-conscious extension of our self. It is a sign that says *This is me. I am here*, and for this to be true forever. The distinguishing mark may simply be the name on the front of a book like my own on this one, an initial in the corner of a painting or an unmistakable personal style.

The art of an artist says, "This is me. I am here", and for this to be true forever

The most popular and durable medium we *artists* use is DNA. In this sense, all mothers and fathers are *artists*. Except that our creations have souls of their own. They are *artists* in their own right.

Pure *artists* are hermaphrodites. We reproduce all by ourselves. We do so through the written word, paint, clay, stone and sound. We live on through the eternal characters we create in novels. We reverberate forever as the combination of notes that make up our songs. We are admired for time immemorial as the unique combination of brushstrokes that form our paintings. Our creations have souls.

Of course, few *artists* get to live on eternally in the

Halls of Fame. Our self-manifestations usually end up in the attic or on the rubbish tip where they decompose over time or fade in the memories of others, like ripples in a pond.

Some *artists* fair rather better. Marilyn Monroe, Gandhi, The Beatles, Hitler, all left an indelible mark. Picasso, who reportedly suffered from acute death anxiety in later life, was among the most prolific *artists,* creating over fifty thousand pieces of self-expression. That is two everyday for over seventy years. As Picasso's biographer and friend John Richardson put it, "by producing images of musketeers, matadors, twisted couples and haunted woman, Picasso was trying to outwit death."

As an *artist*, you, too, can outwit death by creating versions of yourself that live forever.

Essentials of Being
Purpose.

8

Romantics

Have you ever fallen in love?

If you are a *romantic*, you have been struck through the heart by one of Cupid's arrows, tipped with a serum so powerful that it split your life in half - a before and an after.

Before being struck you restlessly wandered through life in search of something but not sure quite what. Then, Bang! You find a missing piece of yourself you did not even know existed so that now, when you stare up at the firmament, instead of futilely wishing upon shooting stars to fill the hole in your being, you connect with every single point in the heavens. Nothing exists that is not a part of you. You are not just in love. You *are* love.

Many search out romantic love. We join dating

agencies, attend dinner parties, frequent clubs and scan supermarket queues for potential soulmates. But romantic love is not something that can be found in the same way as a lost pair of keys. You can't get in the way of a dart through the heart. Romantic love is something that happens *to* you whether you want it to or not.

Some people try to explain romantic love away. Evolutionary psychologists like Helen Fisher propose that the "insanity of love" is the product of a built-in irrationality mechanism in the brain that ensures loyalty to one "co-parent" in order that relationships last long enough for a child to be raised. In other words, romantic love is the product of neurally active chemicals. Love is a drug.

Relationship therapists and gurus believe that romantic love is far from a blind chemical reaction. On the contrary, they propose that we choose those we fall in love with. That each of us has an unconscious capacity to scan another person's psychological blueprint in search of a match. What we are looking for is someone with the same unacknowledged fears, anxieties and coping strategies, but with different ways to cope with them. This serves one of two purposes. Either we can learn from each other, grow and evolve, or we can conspire with our other half to keep our anxieties hidden.

For example, two people who share issues with dependency and trust become a couple in which one is the parent and the other the child. (The "parent" is able to deny their own needs for dependency as they are acted out by their partner, and the "child" can remain insecure, dependent and needy because their partner will look after them). A couple that share issues about control and authority may enter a master/slave relationship. Couples afraid of intimacy become distancers and pursuers, or create emotional war zones by arguing incessantly over everything. Couples with issues around competition may become idols and worshippers. Couples that want to keep anything bad out of their perfect relationship join forces by wearing the same clothes and sharing the same interests.

Of course, even if romantic love can be explained away, the most ardent cynics still fall hopelessly and inexorably in love. They melt like ice and boil with jealousy just like everyone else. Romantic love is like a virus against which no-one can be immunised and for which there is no cure.

Romantics among us who have had our soulmates wrenched away from us spend our whole lives trying to recapture the magic. Like treasure hunters with an old map and a cross marking the spot, we wander through life like wounded heroes, paying homage to our love and singing along to songs like *Endless Love*, *Forever and Always* and *My Heart Will Go On*.

Gladly, we believe, would we sacrifice our lives for our true loves, just like Leonardo DiCaprio in *The Titanic* when he sank to the bottom of the icy waters to save his lover, Kate Winslet.

Romantic love not only awakens the hero in us. It also inspires the poet, prompting us to scratch our initials on tree trunks or recite sublime verses like the following from Robert Ingersoll: "Love is the magician, the enchanter, that changes worthless things to Joy, and makes royal kings and queens of common clay. It is the perfume of the most wondrous flower, the heart, and without that sacred passion, that divine swoon, we are less than beasts; but with it, earth is heaven and we are gods."

Romantic love defies death

Even if love does defy death, I am not suggesting that we fall in love to avoid our fear of death. For a start, one cannot choose to be a *romantic*. Falling in love is like winning the lottery, except that the chances of it happening are extremely high. And when it happens we forget about our aloneness and separateness. We feel whole. We belong. We feel special. Our life has meaning, purpose and hope. We are invincible.

While in love, you are invincible. Your love defies death.

Essential of being
Belonging, specialness, physical intimacy, meaning, purpose and hope.

9

Time Travellers

Do you like planning ahead, reminiscing about the past or replaying fantasies in your mind?

To be a *time traveller* you do not need a time machine to squeeze you through a door in the fabric of the universe to the past and the future. Your physical co-ordinates never change. It is your memory and imagination that traverse space and time.

We all occasionally take a trip down memory lane or fantasise about how wonderful our futures will be. Dedicated *time travellers*, though, spend almost no time at all in the here and now. We live perpetually in our heads, always somewhere else. If you are one of us, a typical day may go something like this.

You begin your day trying to regain the thread of a dream you half remember and which slips from your

The Art of Being Human

grasp as soon as your eyes open. Instead of focusing on the ceiling or the wall, you imagine yourself getting up and making breakfast. When you physically act out these thoughts, you do so on autopilot, your mind focusing instead on the things you have to do during the day and, before you know it, you are sitting down, washed, dressed and slurping coffee or tea in front of the TV. On the screen, images of a family whose home has been washed away by a flood in an exotic country the other side of the world makes you feel sad. Then the news presenter switches your attention to a crime committed by a banker and your mood instantly changes to one of indignation. This feeling is soon replaced by desire and curiosity when the photo of an extremely beautiful or handsome celebrity flickers on the screen.

Your mood abruptly changes yet again when the phone rings. A friend wants to meet for coffee and you discuss potential places to meet. Each time one of you makes a suggestion, you pull up an image of the cafe from your memory, as if going through the pages of a photo album, until you find one you both like.

When you put the phone down you glance at the time and realise you are running late. This makes you panic slightly, prompting a fantasy in which you miss the bus or get a parking ticket, which makes you panic a little bit more. You slurp down the rest of your coffee or tea, head towards the door, return for the keys you forgot and leave again.

Thus passes half an hour of a typical *time traveller's* morning. Not a second did you spend in the here and now. The breakfast you ate, you did not really enjoy. The bitterness or sweetness of your tea or coffee, you did not really savour. The clock you glanced at, you did not hear ticking. While on the phone, you were not conscious of the itch behind your ear or even that you were scratching it. The people on the TV whom you felt sorry for and angry at, you have probably never met nor ever will. Of the stillness of the picture hanging on the wall, you were completely oblivious.

As a *time traveller*, things that happen in the here and now pass by unnoticed, just as time passes unperceived. Tastes, textures and even sounds, you sense without really being aware of them. You are always somewhere else. The reality of things escapes you because you live in a world of memories and imaginings that are all created and controlled in your mind. You select and reinterpret memories. You construct your futures and direct your fantasies to play themselves out exactly how you want them to. You exist in places where reality holds no sway.

Only in the present do the laws of nature apply. Only in actual time do objects exist. Only in the moment does anyone die. While remembering the past, you are always youthful and full of energy. While planning your future, death is just an idea. In your fantasies, you are a superman and superwoman.

And the past and the future is where we *time travellers* exist, continually diverting our attention away from the present by embroiling ourselves in stories in which we win the lottery, give the perfect put-down, humble our enemies and seduce the people we most desire. As the nineteenth century French philosopher Blaise Pascal said, "we are only truly happy when daydreaming about future happiness."

As time travellers we divert our attention away from the present where reality and death exist

Existentialists take this notion of time travelling a step further. They reason that to act at all we must project ourselves into the future. If you want to make a paper aeroplane, for example, you must first imagine or remember what a paper aeroplane looks like, otherwise you would end up with a crunched ball of paper, unless you happen to be extremely lucky.

Take this idea a step further and a more worrying possibility arises. If you were unable to remember the past or project yourself into the future, you would be as good as dead in that you would not be aware of your existence. You would exist in the same way that a tree or a rock exists. You would just be. Death, in this sense, is *not* being able to remember or imagine.

Fortunately, there is a past and a future, and we *time travellers* spend an awful lot of time in it.

As a habitual *time traveller*, you exist where death cannot reach you.

Essentials of Being

Purpose and control.

10

Reflections

Do you invest in anti-ageing products or have a partner who is a lot younger than you?

When you get up in the morning and peer at yourself in the mirror on the wall, the image reflected back at you is a true representation of how you look. You may not feel the same way every morning about what you see, but the mirror never lies.

Not all mirrors, of course, are inanimate plates of glass and metal amalgam. Our self-image is also reflected back at us through the eyes of others. Social psychologists have long since considered that how we perceive ourselves is largely determined by how the world perceives us. In other words, we construct our identities on the basis of others' attitudes towards us. For example, if you believe you are beautiful it is because the world around you treats you as someone beautiful. You fit the particular stereotype of beauty applicable to the part of the world you live in at the time you live in it. Likewise, if you admire or despise yourself, at the root of your self-esteem is usually an experience of someone else's negative or positive perception of you.

We all collude with this subjectivity. If you think you do not, why bother putting on your smart clothes before going to a job interview or tidying your home before receiving guests?

The extent to which our self-perception is determined by the world around us is brought into stark relief by those of us who live in countries where values are markedly different from our own. When we walk down the street, the image we have of ourselves is no longer confirmed or reinforced, so we exaggerate our characteristics, sometimes to the extent of parodying ourselves. A trip down to the Costa del Sol will clarify this.

Of course, just as we see ourselves through the eyes of the world, so we can tell the world what to see. We can deceive the mirror.

Just as we see ourselves through the eyes of the world, so we tell the world what to see

One of the most common deceptions is to convince the mirror that we are younger than we actually are. As a *reflection* living in the twenty-first century this is not particularly difficult, especially if you are a woman. At your disposal you have a myriad of products and procedures that enable you to deceive the mirror - aka yourself and the world around you. They include hair dyes and implants, anti-wrinkle and firming creams, botox, chin tucks and tummy tucks. You can even have your whole face peeled off and replaced with a wrinkle-free one.

Traditionally, men employ other ways to deceive the mirror. One of the most common is reflected in the old pun, *I am as young as the woman I feel.* In other words, women are men's self-reflections. Tom Cruise, either by coincidence or unconscious design, is a classic example of someone with the potential to benefit from such a deception. When he was still a young man his first wife, Mimi Rogers, was six years older than him. His second wife, Nicole Kidman, was five years his junior. As he reached mid-life, his third significant partner, Penélope Cruz, was twelve years younger. His fourth, Katie Holmes, is sixteen years younger.

Whether you are a twenty-first century woman or man, the myriad of anti-ageing products available and the slackening of social taboos means that deceiving the mirror is relatively easy. Still, it is a subtle art. It is one thing to have a facelift. It is altogether another to have five facelifts. Likewise, cavorting with someone who is three-quarters your age may be socially acceptable, but seducing someone less than half your age may not be. In the eyes of the world a line exists that once crossed, turns you into a sad clown or worse.

Why give into people's prejudices, though? You are as old as you feel and, if you are like most *reflections*, your mind always feels somewhere between eight and eighteen years old. You are not deceiving anyone. You are simply correcting the assumption that your body determines your age.

If you have mastered the art of being a *reflection*, you can seem forever young.

Essentials of Being
Control.

11

Biological Immortals

Will this chapter pique your curiosity enough for you to want to find out more?

Have you ever thought about living forever? Not just in a spiritual or hypothetical sense, but to really live forever. To extend *this* life, as yourself, with your present awareness, identity and memories. To be biologically immortal.

Others may consider those of us who contemplate such a possibility to be either wacky professors or delusional egomaniacs with more money than sense.

We are not. The fact of the matter is that *biological immortals* already exist. Real, living, breathing organisms that can live forever. One such creature is a jellyfish called *Turritopsis nutricula*. Through a cell conversion process called transdifferentiation, this aquatic animal reverts to being a child every time it becomes a sexually mature adult - a cycle that repeats itself forever or until disease, trauma or hungry predators cut short the jellyfish's immortality.

True, you are not jellyfish and the only humans to have discovered the fabled *elixir of eternal youth* are fictional characters like Indiana Jones, Dracula and Elves.

Yet the *elixir of eternal youth* is within your grasp. Life extensionists even know how it will stop the process of ageing. Here is a bit of science to clarify exactly how. Ageing, or senescence as it is called, occurs because the cells that make up our being, our DNA, stop dividing and die. This happens because at the end of each cell exists a little cap called a telomere. Each time the cell divides, this little cap gets shorter and shorter until eventually it disappears altogether and the cell is unable to divide, and so dies. Some cells, however, such as cancer cells and stem cells produce an enzyme called telomerase that helps the telomere grow again, enabling the cell to divide forever and therefore live forever. (This is one of the reasons that finding a cure for cancer is so difficult). For the *elixir of eternal youth*, all that is needed is to find a way to make this enzyme work on healthy cells.

So, you see, the potential for biological immortality already exists and there are plenty of neuroscientists and biochemists working to realise such a dream. Some life-extension advocates say that it is a matter of decades, not centuries, before the breakthrough.

When the time does come, unlike the immortal jellyfish, you will not have to worry about being killed by a virus or nasty bacteria. Nanotechnology will have sufficiently advanced to pump into your bloodstream lots of little nanorobots, programmed to seek and destroy anything vaguely dangerous like cancer cells.

Alternatively, you will be able to use advancements in cyborgology to have your consciousness uploaded onto a computer or placed in a robotic life-support system. You will even be able to programme your own experiences, just like in *The Matrix* and *Vanilla Sky*.

Admittedly, these technologies are not available right now. Fear not, though. You can wait as long as it takes by signing up to modern cryonics, a procedure which uses a process called vitrification to freeze your body into a glass-like state. This technology is readily available and reasonably priced for anyone with a nest egg: only thirty thousand dollars for cryopreservation of your brain and around one hundred and forty thousand dollars for your whole body, plus a bit extra for a "standby team" that can begin the procedure at your bedside.

Of course, there are some ethical issues. What about God, the afterlife and reincarnation? If you take an evolutionist's perspective, you need not worry about such considerations. Biological immortality was probably one of the many evolutionary steps that occurred and was not selected because species that live forever do not multiply at a quick-enough rate to evolve and adapt to the changing environment. Immortals are simply not as successful at surviving as mortals are.

If you ever succeed in becoming biologically immortal, you will not need to fear death because there is a good chance you will never have to face it. Not your own, anyway.

Essentials of Being
Permanence and hope.

12

Trippers

Do you use a mood altering substance on a daily basis?

If you are a *tripper*, you feel existential angst just like everyone else, only how anxious you feel is not solely influenced by your genetic make-up, past experiences, present circumstances and future expectations. You have an *extra something* that makes being terminally human that little bit more manageable. Your sunsets are more beautiful, strangers less threatening, dancing more liberating, hazardous journeys more relaxing and the spectra of death less menacing.

This *extra something* grows naturally in the wild and can be manufactured in laboratories. It can be taken in the form of a pill or a powder, a drink or an intravenous cocktail. It can be swallowed, sniffed, snorted, inhaled and absorbed. It has medical names, nicknames and code names. It is illegally sold on street corners, legally prescribed by doctors and clandestinely shared out by Shamans.

If you are a *tripper*, you take drugs.

Depending on your disposition, lifestyle and anxiety levels, you have an array of hallucinogens, deliriants and anti-anxiety drugs to choose from. Here are some you may have tried or been prescribed: magic mushrooms, peyote, ecstasy, marijuana, opium, Xanax, Valium, Prozac and Zoloft.

To be a *tripper*, you do not need to know how your drugs work. Then again, it really is quite simple. They either slow down or speed up your central nervous system. If you are curious to know exactly how, here is a more detailed explanation.

Hallucinogens like peyote, magic mushrooms, LSD and ecstasy work by binding with a type of serotonin receptor in the brain that facilitates the transmission of nerve impulses. When a hallucinogenic compound binds with serotonin receptors, serotonin is blocked and nerve transmission is altered. The increase in free, unbound serotonin in the brain results in a distortion in time and space, alterations of mood and synesthesia - the "seeing" of sounds and the "hearing" of colours.

Other side effects include flashbacks, reduced inhibition, increased empathy, mellowness and feelings of bliss.

Anti-anxiety drugs such as the benzodiazepines Xanax and Valium, as well as tranquillisers, work by slowing down the central nervous system.

Antidepressants such as Prozoc and Zoloft are also prescribed for generalised anxiety and panic disorders and work by increasing serotonin in the brain and decreasing dopamine.

Beta blockers, usually prescribed to treat high blood pressure and heart problems, are also prescribed for anxiety. They work by blocking the effects of norepinephrine, a stress hormone involved in the fight-or-flight response. This helps control the physical symptoms of anxiety such as rapid heart rate, trembling voice, sweating, dizziness and shaky hands.

No drug has yet been found or manufactured that provides an anxiety-free existence all the time. Until then, drugs provide relief from anxiety, not a cure.

As a *tripper*, existential angst seeps out that little bit less, so long as you keep taking the pills.

Essentials of Being
Control.

13

Procrastinators

Do you put off making decisions and avoid commitments?

If you are a *procrastinator*, you have something that decisive individuals must relinquish - the freedom that comes with unlimited choice. As a *procrastinator*, you do not allow yourself to be tied down by commitments and promises you cannot keep. You keep your options open. You leave your doors ajar.

Everyone begins with unlimited choice. Just getting peckish opens up a whole world of possibilities. For example, do you prepare a meal, buy a ready-made one, order a takeaway or go out to eat?

Economics, availability, mobility, cultural norms, past experience, the weather, the occasion, how hungry you are, your mood, personal preferences and the number of people you usually eat with will all either curtail or broaden your options.

For the sake of simplicity and to keep this example short, let us agree that you are at home alone and have nothing in the fridge. Let us also agree that you have no car, live in a medium-sized town on a medium salary and that you are feeling too lazy to prepare a meal, face a trip to the supermarket or do any washing up. So you plump for the easiest option - a takeaway.

Still, there are choices to be made. What kind of takeaway? Chinese? Indian? Thai? Pizza? Again, you opt for the one with least choices: a pizza. Browsing through the directory, you are confronted with various takeaway services. You close your eyes and order from the one your finger lands on. Still, there are a variety of pizzas for you to choose from, at least five of which you like. You select the one you usually have, turn on the TV, sit down and wait.

Thus ends the chain of choices that being hungry set into motion. When the pizza finally arrives, you slip into old habits that require little conscious decision making such as eating, brushing your teeth, undressing, slipping into bed and drifting off to sleep, where conscious choice eludes you altogether.

What does all this have to do with avoiding

existential angst? Well, while awake and aware, each time we make a choice we must renounce something and each time we renounce something we remind ourselves that life is limited. If, for example, you finally plumped for a Margarita pizza, you spurned all the others on the menu. You renounced the Chinese and the Indian, rejected the ready-made meal for one at the supermarket and forewent the chance to eat out alone in a McDonald's or fish & chip shop. In other words, for every *yes* there is a *no*. Every time you choose something, you lose something.

Of course, by committing to a pizza we sacrifice very little because there will be other times when we feel peckish. Everything we gave up will be available next time we feel hungry.

When it comes to big decisions and commitments, it is a different matter altogether. Decisions like buying or selling a house and planning next year's holiday. Commitments like long-term relationships and mortgages. Unlike lunch, the things we relinquish we may be relinquishing forever. When we choose a wife or a husband, we agree never to sleep with anyone else again. When we embark on a career path, we sacrifice every other career. Each time we make a decision we experience a loss. When we sell a home we lose the life we lived there. When we break up a relationship, we lose that person in our lives. When we book a holiday, we sign up to experiencing the end of the holiday when we say goodbye to places and people we will probably never see again.

Not so for we *procrastinators*. We have a host of strategies that ensure there is no end to the number of choices at our disposal. We avoid relinquishment and loss.

The most common strategy is to put off committing to anything long term altogether. We dabble in life. We become serial monogamists, we rent our living spaces and keep our diaries free.

Another strategy we *procrastinators* employ is to do the opposite of planning. We let circumstances and whims determine our next move. Like rudderless boats guided by the winds of fate we are not giving up anything because anything can happen.

For clever *procrastinators* and the superrich, we avoid relinquishment and loss by possessing and experiencing everything all of the time. We commit to long-term relationships but secretly break their rules by having affairs. Instead of buying one house in one place, we buy two or three or four in different places.

How does procrastinating and having unlimited

choice help keep existential anxiety at bay? Well, each choice we make is a boundary experience that confronts us with the limits of possibility and with our own finiteness. By not choosing and not committing, we avoid these boundary experiences.

Like death, every decision we make confronts us with the limits of possibility and with our own finiteness

In the words of the existential psychotherapist Irvin Yalom, "The more we face our limits, the more we have to relinquish our myth of personal specialness, unlimited potential, imperishability and immunity to the laws of nature."

As a *procrastinator*, you rarely have to deal with your fear of death because you rarely have to confront your own finiteness.

Essentials of Being
Freedom and hope.

14

Threesomes

Do you see yourself as a victim, saviour or persecutor?

In almost every story there lurks a victim, a persecutor and a saviour. In fairy tales of yonder year, the victim is a damsel in distress, the persecutor a fire-eating dragon and the saviour a knight in shining armour. In westerns such as *The Magnificent Seven*, the victim is a village of peaceful peasants, the persecutors a gang of baddies and the saviours a gang of goodies. In horror stories like Dracula, it is a virgin, a vampire and a love-struck priest.

Although you are probably not a damsel in distress, vampire or gunslinger, the drama triangle plays itself out in almost all of your relationships. You have only to suspect your partner of having an affair and immediately, you take on the role of victim and your partner's lover that of persecutor.

Relationships, of course, are more complex than fairy tales and films. Depending on which side of the fence you sit, victims can be persecutors and saviours victims. If, for example, your partner really were having an affair, it could be that they felt hurt or neglected by you, in which case they are your victim and the new person in their life their saviour. Likewise, in territorial conflicts when militant groups are freedom fighters, they are saviours, but as terrorists, they are persecutors. It is all relative.

So, when you ask yourself the question, *Am I a victim, persecutor or saviour?* no single answer can be true all the time. You oscillate between roles or simultaneously take on all three. One minute, for example, you are the victim of an injustice, like an unwarranted parking fine and the next you become the perpetrator because you are unloading your frustration onto the innocent, local authority telephone operator.

That said, you may associate more with one role than another. If life seems to conspire against you and luck never seems to be on your side, you probably see yourself as one of life's *victims*. If others tend to perceive you as a *persecutor*, you are probably simply a victim avenging injustices that have been committed against you. If you find yourself constantly rescuing people, you are probably a *saviour*.

What has being a *victim, persecutor* or *saviour* got to do with avoiding our most primordial fear? Well, implicit in each role is the promise of escape from the thing we most fear. Ingrained in *victims* is the belief that we will be rescued. As *persecutors* we transfer our fear onto our victims. As *saviours* we always triumph over the *persecutor*.

Obviously, *victims* do not believe they will actually be saved from death. *Persecutors* know that they are not the grim reaper in person. *Saviours* know they cannot slay death. Yet, on a subtle, unconscious level, by participating in the drama triangle we hold onto the promise of escape.

The drama triangle is the triangle of life. Only by participating in it can you experience love, hate, joy, desire, fear, anger and relief. Elude it and you will feel very little. You will be as good as dead.

Essentials of Being
Hope.

15

Know-it-alls

Are you an obsessive tidier, an ardent puzzle solver or a control freak?

If you are a *know-it-all*, you like to understand things. You crave explanations and order. You derive a certain pleasure from putting things in their place, filing and categorising things. You like to work things out to their logical conclusion. You enjoy putting the last piece in the jigsaw or completing the crossword. Your house is tidy and your book shelves ordered by size and category. You own maps, calculators and rulers. You watch documentaries about the natural world and how it works. Before going on holiday, you may even check the weather forecast and flight departure times. You thirst for knowledge and when you do not know something or feel uncertain, you look it up in your encyclopaedia or google it.

In other words, you abhor not knowing, disorder and uncertainty. You feel overly anxious when a football result hangs in the balance. You get tetchy and frustrated when you do not understand what someone is trying to say. You get unreasonably irritated when you cannot find the lid of the pen you are using.

Knowing and being certain about things makes us feel safe

Most of us *know-it-alls* obsess about the little everyday things in our lives. Some *know-it-alls*, like the TOE physicists, want to order and understand the whole of existence. They want to produce the so called *Theory of Everything* which, in the words of the cosmologist Stephen Hawking, will enable us to "know the mind of God."

Apparently, all that is required for this *Theory of Everything* is to unite the general theory of relativity that explains and predicts the behaviour of everything big with quantum mechanics that explains the behaviour of everything tiny. Presently the two theories are inconsistent with one another.

Evolutionists already claim to know how life

evolved. Still, they cannot answer the big question, *Where did life come from?* By chance in a primordial soup or through divine intervention?

Current understanding of the TOE physicists is that in the beginning there was perfect unity. Nothing existed except the unbroken wholeness of the superforce. There was no matter, no particles, no gravity, no electromagnetism and no weak and strong nuclear forces. This perfection reigned for a mere split second because the violent explosion of Creation caused the budding universe to expand. The four forces split. Energy coalesced into matter and particles joined to form atoms, which slowly congregated into vast clouds. Over aeons these clouds condensed into galaxies, stars, planets, you and I.

In short, the perfect wholeness of the superforce fragmented. What exists now are the broken shards of this symmetry. The shattered pieces of an original "perfect" unity. Everything has become muddled, murky and messy.

If you are a *know-it-all*, you may not be an expert on, or even have the slightest interest in, general relativity, quantum mechanics, singularities and multi-dimensional hyper-spheres. But something inside you makes you want to replicate this original symmetry, even if it is just nudging into place an askew picture, placing the ornament on the shelf equidistant from the others, straightening a carpet so that it is flush with the wall, or colour-coding your CD collection. You want your world to be comprehensible, ordered, predictable and under control.

As a *know-it-all*, being sure about everything and having everything under control cushions you from the existential angst that comes from not knowing, chaos and uncertainty.

Essentials of being
Control.

16

Happy Enders

Do you like block busters and best sellers?

If you are a *happy ender*, you like happy endings. That is not to say you have ever experienced a happy ending first hand. You certainly have never sailed off into the sunset arm in arm with you lover, never to be seen or heard of again. You may have sailed off somewhere but, once out at sea, a storm will have broken, the wind dropped or a petty argument will have ensued over who left the mobile phone charger behind.

Your endings, like everyone else's, simply separate one chunk of time from another. They are the significant moments in your life that you stick into your family albums: You waving bye-bye as you embark on your first trip away. You on your wedding day. You outside your new house. You with your newborn baby. You receiving an award or holding a trophy aloft. You at the top of a mountain.

Such moments are certainly happy, but they are not endings. They mark the end of chapters and episodes, after which there are more chapters and episodes in which other things happen: Your baby grows up. The house you bought, you sell. Your victory in the local competition is followed by defeat. No happy ending is final for those who go on living.

The only "real" happy endings take place in books and films. Only in these fictitious worlds do the lovers who sail off into the sunset never return, because the last page and the last scene really are the last ones. The lovers exist within defined parameters outside of which they cannot exist. When the boat disappears from view over the horizon, there is no other horizon. The lovers' passionate kiss in the final scene is not followed by a trip to the toilet. There is no *to be continued...*

We *happy enders* spend a lot of time reading books and watching films that contain "real" happy endings. We read crime novels in which the culprit is always caught. We devour whodunnits in which the mystery is always solved. We watch westerns in which revenge is always exacted. We are entranced by romantic comedies in which the lovers always reunite against all odds. We follow adventures in which the treasure is always found.

There are only a handful of popular books and films in which the end is not a happy one. *Death in Venice* is one of them. Set in Venice just before an impending plague, it relates the tragic story of a middle-aged writer who has been ravaged by loss and whose tired body no longer attracts the admirers he desires.

The ageing dandy's yearning for his lost youth becomes even more poignant when he finds himself inextricably drawn towards a young adolescent male. In an attempt to seduce the boy, the protagonist pays a visit to a local barber where he has his hair dyed and face rouged to give him the illusion of youth.

The film reaches its finale when the freshly made-up dandy follows the youth to a beach and, seating himself in a deck chair, watches the young boy wade into the ocean, gaze towards the horizon and then turn, arm outstretched as if beckoning. Desperately, the ageing dandy tries to get up and follow the angelic apparition, but suffers a fatal heart attack and slumps back into the chair, his hair dye and make-up streaming down his face.

Such endings are not much in demand among *happy enders*, and most novelists and almost the entire film industry dutifully caters for our need for a *happy ever after*. Mysteries are never left unsolved. Villains never escape and heroes never die unless it is a selfless act of love for some higher purpose. The goodies always win, the baddies always loose and we close the book or leave the cinema with the warm, satisfied inner glow of someone who knows that all ends well.

As a *happy ender*, etched deep into your unconscious is the belief that all endings are happy, including your own.

Essentials of Being
Hope.

A Therapist's View II

If you have reflected on the sixteen *identities* in this book, more than one of them will have provoked a smile of recognition, half-suppressed perhaps or still lingering. Those that did not may have stirred a memory of some younger you, or may lie-in-wait for events and circumstances to prompt an older, future self to discover new ways of being.

Some of the *identities* you may view as desperate attempts to enhance reality, like beautiful flares luring our attention away from the darkness of being, or beacons of hope emanating from our desire for life. Others you may regard as scientific facts, spiritual truths or psychological realities. Or mere conjecture even.

Whatever your point of view, the beliefs, alliances and ways of behaving that form our *identities* provide us with the *essentials of being* we need to feel safe and alive: a sense of permanence, specialness, belonging, physical intimacy, control, meaning, purpose and hope.

For those of us who manage to sustain a combination of *identities* that together provide us with all the *essentials of beings*, existential angst does not generally pierce the surface. Those of us who struggle to integrate into our life these *essentials of being* find it more difficult to keep our fear of death at bay - especially if our *identities* have been threatened or thwarted at some time in our lives.

A prolonged absence of some *essentials of being* such as meaning, purpose and hope can even lead to despair and the kind of self-destructive behaviour that causes the very death we originally feared.

To keep existential anxiety at bay we nurture a combination of identities that together provide us with the essentials of being we need to feel safe and alive

We have all had our *identities* threatened to some extent, whether it be our physical bodies that have been ravaged by illness or time, our emotions that have been traumatised by humiliation or neglect, or our spirit that has been riddled with doubt and guilt. For those among us whose wounds have yet to heal, existential angst seeps out of the cracks in our being and we feel more vulnerable when we receive subsequent blows to our *identities*.

Existential anxiety seeps out of unhealed wounds

Even if our wounds are superficial, rarely do any of us feel happy or at peace for any significant length of time. More often than not, we are caught up in the battle between our multiple *identities* as they fight for supremacy and survival, not because our multiple *identities* are enemies but because the beliefs, alliances and behaviour they embody naturally conflict with one another.

If, for example, you have a *special one* in your entourage of *identities*, for your *special one* to maintain its uniqueness it naturally clashes with *identities* that want to conform and imitate in order to belong, such as a *member* or *brand*. Likewise, if one of your *identities* requires intuition and faith to survive, such as a *believer* or *spiritualist*, it naturally locks horns with your *identities* that need logic and control to exist, such as *know-it-alls* and *biological immortals*.

Our multiple identities naturally conflict with one another

One of the strategies battling *identities* use to dominate one another is self-sabotage. If, for example, your *special one* wants to go it alone in the world of business, it will try to sabotage any attempts of your *member* to become a "cog in the wheel" of a big company. Your *special one* may do this by having you forget to send off the job application form or by blurting out something inappropriate in the interview.

Not that your conscious mind is always aware of your self-sabotaging. It happens below the surface of your awareness, at an unconscious level.

If one of your *identities* succeeds in dominating, it tries to disown the others by either driving them inside and repressing them or expelling them into the external world and projecting them onto other people who can more easily be attacked and vilified.

If, for example, you have a particularly powerful and pious *believer identity*, it will either try to repress the carnal desires of your *player* self or support a world in which your *player's* animalistic behaviour is forbidden, punished and controlled.

When one identity dominates, it represses or expels the others

However dominant an *identity* becomes, its repressed desires and needs cannot be denied for long. Inevitably, they burst out as uncontrollable, pent up emotion or manifest as skin complaints, tiredness, headaches and impotence. Likewise, *identities* that we project onto others invariably return to haunt us. If you particularly dislike someone for no apparent reason, it is often because they represent a part of yourself you are reluctant to acknowledge.

Even when an *identity* does succeed in dominating, it cannot sustain itself in isolation for long. A dominant *special one* ultimately suffers from isolation and loneliness. A dominant *member* becomes frustrated by its inability to control the fate of the group to which it belongs and regrets not striding out on its own. Dominating *believers* are plagued by guilt and shame or haunted by the fear of hellfire and karmic retribution. *Spiritualists* who "wake up" in the dream become dissociated, or an inflation of the self makes them believe they are further along the path than they really are. *Players* in the Game of Life who take time out to reflect on the meaning of their existence, realise that in the grand scheme of things there really is none. Dominant *artists* lose themselves in their creations and become increasingly incapable of distinguishing between themselves and the external world, just like children. Hopeless *romantics* are consumed by jealousy. *Time travellers* disconnect with their authentic self because it is just not as exciting as their remembered and imagined one. *Reflections* are shocked by the apparent passing of twenty years overnight when they finally cease to apply their creams and hair dyes. Addicted *trippers* suffer from an array of side effects including delirium, hostility, depersonalisation, uncontrollable impulsive behaviour, insomnia, suicidal thoughts, depression and psychosis. *Procrastinators* discover that by avoiding commitments they have become tourists in their own lives. *Know-it-alls* become trapped in their own cold and calculating prisons. The expectations of *happy enders* are dashed on the rocks of reality.

If we desperately attempt to cling to a single *identity*, our beliefs, alliances and behaviour become ever more exaggerated, fantastic and unsustainable, leading us to depression and delusions of grandeur.

Desperate attempts to cling to single identities leads to evermore exaggerated and unsustainable beliefs

One way to avoid the inevitable internal conflict that stems from self-sabotage, repression and denial is to create parallel bubble worlds in which our multiple *identities* can live independently from one another, each with its own set of friends, haunts, clothes, language and even names. Our *special one* secretly tiptoes around our head, or metamorphoses as a light warrior in an online fantasy world. Our hedonistic *player* struts its stuff at bars, clubs and in sleazy hotel rooms.

Of course, we cannot hide our *identities* from ourselves, unless we happen to have a particularly severe multiple personality disorder, but we can hide them from everyone else. We can ensure that our different sets of friends do not mix. We can provide each of our *identities* with its own phone number, password, membership card and secret hideaway.

Leading parallel lives is no easy ride, though. It requires a good deal of imagination, planning and deception because when two worlds collide, like bubbles, they tend to burst - as illicit lovers caught in the act know only too well.

To avoid self-sabotage and denial we lead duplicitous lives

How anxious we feel on an existential level is not, then, merely determined by how many *essentials of being* we integrate into our lives. It also depends on how we deal with the inevitable conflict that arises because of their natural incompatibility.

One brave and ultimately rewarding way to avoid the inevitable fragmentation of the self that arises out of self-sabotage, denial and duplicity is to learn how to simultaneously embrace the opposing desires and needs of our multiple *identities*. In other words, to believe and to doubt at the same time. To think both intuitively and logically. To forge your own path without breaking ties with your group. To commit to relationships without sacrificing your independence. To live in the here and now while chasing your dream. To simultaneously embrace certainty and uncertainty. To honour equally your body, your mind and your spirit. To allow your imagination to soar while keeping your feet firmly planted on the ground.

To reduce internal conflict we must learn to embrace simultaneously opposing thoughts and desires

A key to enjoying our search for this precarious balance of opposing forces is to accept that there is no end to our journey; no final resting place we can enjoy and relax in for any prolonged period of time - not while alive, anyway. Sustained balance, wholeness, and inner peace are beyond us because they are the consequence of imbalance, fragmentation and conflict. Without feeling hungry you cannot enjoy feeling full. Without desire you cannot bask in the peace that follows release. Without fear you cannot let out a sigh of relief. Without one cigarette you cannot crave the next from which you draw your comfort. Peace, the psychological equivalent of inertia, requires war.

Even if you do, momentarily, achieve an undisturbed state of non-desire or homeostasis, it never lasts long. Sooner rather than later an image, a smell, a caress or the twinkle in someone's eye rekindles your desire or triggers your fear, and off you go again on your pursuit of peace and happiness.

Some of us even deliberately create more conflict in our lives, stretching our emotional elastic band to the limit so that our release is more intense and our sigh of release more profound. We break up with our lovers so that we can feel the full power of the embrace when we reunite. In bed, we allow ourselves to be tied up and teased. We walk on the edge of love and life.

Others among us try to minimise the tension in our lives. We endeavour to get closer to peace for longer. We visit counsellors and therapists to resolve conflict, or we simply avoid the stimuli that creates it. We meditate under trees. We distance ourselves from those that tempt and provoke us. We retreat from life.

Lasting peace between warring identities is unattainable

Even if we do manage to negotiate a precarious balance between our warring *identities*, anxiety over the precariousness of existence still spills over into our awareness and our dreams. Storms on life's ocean of uncertainty break whether we like it or not and the corpse we carry in our cargo slides about, reminding us of the shipwreck that awaits.

These emotional storms take place periodically

throughout everyone's life. They mount during adolescence when we depart the sanctuary of our home and family. They break when grey hairs announce that we have passed half way. Wind tears at our sails when loved ones are torn away from us. Lightning strikes when we suffer a heart attack, have a stroke or contract a terminal disease.

And if it is not you who is caught in the storm, just turn on the TV and you are forced to bear witness to hoards of humans sinking to the bottom of life's ocean because of a bomb, an earthquake or a huge wave. None of them woke up that day with the slightest inkling it would be their last. Just like you this morning.

However safe we feel, anxiety about our existence spills into our everyday lives

How destructive or constructive these storms are depends on our ability to heal old wounds, to nurture the *identities* that keep our fear of death at bay and, ultimately, on our courage when the time comes to confront our fear.

One of the keys to achieving this is self-awareness. By being self-aware we are able to acknowledge the wounds through which our anxiety seeps and decide on how best to heal them.

Being aware of which *identities* provide us with our *essentials of being* allows us to nurture the ones we have and develop those we lack.

Being mindful that a time will come when we are no longer self-aware enables us to act in accordance with this eventuality: to heal rifts and tie up the loose ends so that when our awareness finally slips under the surface, rather than leave behind shards of anger and regret floating on the surface, we create little ripples of loving kindness that wash over our family and friends.

In other words, in the battle with an unassailable enemy, there are times we must retreat and administer to our wounds, times when we must avoid the enemy and a time when we must confront it

Regardless of how well we administer to our wounds, however harmonious our *identities* are and however brave we are in the face of death, to really feel alive requires feeling vibrantly connected to those around us and to the planet we inhabit. To love and feel loved. To not feel alone.

To achieve this we must be able to empathise with and feel compassion towards one another. It is my belief, and the message of this book, that one way to improve our chances of this is to acknowledge that beyond the beliefs, alliances and behaviour that traditionally separate us dwells a common fear that unites us on a quest to outwit the same unassailable foe - one we can neither see, feel, negotiate with or kill.

> *Whatever flags we fly, we are all sailing towards the same inevitable yet unknowable end*

After all, as creatures of time, that which separates us from another is merely the consequence of circumstance. You may well hold in your hands the "truth" or the "facts", but it is still your geographical co-ordinates in time and space that have prompted you to adopt them.

If you support a football team, for example, did you really choose your particular team, or did your team choose you because of a combination of the following circumstances over which you had little or no control? 1.) You enjoyed football in your youth or spent time with someone who did. 2.) People you admired or wanted to be associated with supported your team. 3.) You spent a period of your life close to your team's home ground. 4.) Your team was very successful at the time you began supporting a team. 5.) Your team's kit happened to coincide with your notion of cool or beautiful.

Change any of the circumstances that prompted you to support your team and you would probably be supporting a different one.

The same reasoning can be applied to any religious beliefs you may hold. If you are a Muslim, Jew, Christian, Hindu or Buddhist, you probably have someone close to you who has handed this belief on. Even if you are an agnostic or an atheist you are likely to have spent some time in a society or in the presence of someone that champions evolution and self-determination.

The flags we fly are determined by circumstance

The fact that your beliefs and alliances are influenced by circumstance does not mean that your science is not correct, that your God is not the only God or that the team you support is not the best. Nor need it diminish your commitment towards them.

A problem arises, however, when the sentiments *I*

believe, *I think* and *I support* become *I hold the only truth*, *I am right* and *my team are always the best*. Not because what you know or believe is not true, but because it really makes little difference. Every belief, alliance and way of behaving serves the same purpose: they provide us with the *essentials of being* we need to feel safe and alive: a sense of permanence, specialness, belonging, physical intimacy, control, meaning, purpose and hope.

Whether life actually has meaning or purpose does not matter. As human beings we need it. Why? Because there is a hole in everyone's awareness, and no matter how much you know, investigate, love, pray, eat or kill, you, too, will fall through it. So far, nobody has returned to tell the tale. Infinity, death and nothingness are beyond us all.

> *Nobody really knows if being human has meaning or purpose, but we all need meaning and purpose*

The art of being human is our expression of how we deal with the uncertainty that comes with this not-knowing. Our artwork is that of dreaming, praying, loving, creating, fornicating and playing.

The Art of Being Human

Part of the joy of being human comes from being able to appreciate this art. To revel in the myriad of ways we deal with not knowing. To appreciate and connect with each person's rhythm as we serenade life on the road to death, all howling at the moon in our own way. To marvel at each person's quirks, idiosyncrasies and local colour, mindful that whether we are seeking the love that makes us whole, cheering our team on to victory, praying to the God that saves us or studying the science that explains us, we are all searching for meaning and purpose while sailing towards the same certain, yet unknowable, end.

A Personal View

The Art of Being Human was born out of my desire to reflect a view of life that I believe can serve as a useful reference for individuals, like myself, who sail on life's ocean of uncertainty in search of meaning and purpose, without wishing to get embroiled in the bloody battle over the "truth".

It is the view that whatever flags we fly, Gods we pray to or science we use to explain ourselves, they are all inspired at some level by our need to banish our fear of the same personal tragedy awaiting us all - our own death.

Although such a view may seem macabre and unnerving, by acknowledging it we come to realise that we have more in common than we thought with people whose beliefs, alliances and behaviour conflict with our own. Rather like when a catastrophe such as a flood or snow storm momentarily tears us away from our own individual pursuit of happiness and unites us in a common humanitarian cause.

I am not suggesting that by recognising that we are all haunted by a tragedy that has yet to happen, we will all start embracing one another, sharing photos of loved ones and handing out sandwiches. I am simply proposing that in our daily battles, when our blood boils and our passions burn, by being mindful that we are all battling with the same fear of the same unassailable enemy, we can deal our blows with a little less malice and a little more compassion.

One could argue that choosing to contemplate such a view is a bit like glimpsing a flash of light while walking through the woods at night and suspecting that it is the glint of an assassin's blade, rather than the glittering of a lover's ring, a shooting star or a divine spark.

However, even though assassins do exist, I would not advise anyone to roam through life fearing that one lurks around every corner. Neither do I put into question the existence of God or doubt in love. The aim of this book is certainly not to heroically stare death in the eye - to confront the assassin, as it were. On the contrary, it is to reflect on how we keep our

A Personal View

fear of our assassin at bay. It is about how we deflect our attention away from death. It is about how we befriend, run and hide from death. How we honour, disguise and even side with death. It is about how, to achieve this, we learn to love and hate, destroy and create, seduce, possess and play. It is about why we strive for success, pray for forgiveness, fight for survival and will our futures into existence. It is about the art of being human.

I have called this perspective on life *a therapist's view* because it provides a recognisable frame for the reader to place themselves in relation to. After all, we all want to know if the book we are reading threatens our beliefs or strengthens them, agrees or disagrees with us. In other words, is it friend or foe?

I would like to think this book, like myself in the role of therapist for my clients, is neither. Rather, that it be viewed as a mirror into which the reader can self-reflect - a mirror which, in theory, is non-judgemental and unbiased and whose purpose is to help the onlooker become authentic and congruent.

By alluding to the fact I am a therapist, I am implying that I know something about the subject of death. I do not. Like everyone else, I simply struggle to deal with it as best I can. What I do know about is how to help people overcome anxiety caused by past traumatic experiences such as loss, abuse, neglect, humiliation or simply an overload of everyday life. In other words, I help stop anxiety caused in the past seep into and distort the present. My first book, *Safe Space*, provides a model and procedure to achieve this.

For this book, I have simply shifted the focus of my gaze towards the future and to how our pending final trauma influences our beliefs and behaviour. Unlike *Safe Space,* this book does not set out to heal old wounds or reduce the flow of anxiety. Death is not something that we can overcome. It is simply a reflection on how we are all connected through our struggle to deal with this fact.

The original working title for this book was *A Therapist's View of Romance, Football, Evolution & Heaven.* It is the same title I use for my lectures on the theme and I include it now as the subtitle for the same reason: to attract as wide a variety of reader as possible. It is certainly more alluring than a more accurate title such as *How we cope with the fact that we are all going to die.* Any allusion to death, especially our own, is an immediate turn-off for most people.

However intriguing or provocative the title of a

book, especially non-fiction, appealing to readers with conflicting world views is extremely difficult. As a reader myself, I am drawn to books that agree with me or expand my view on subjects that interest me. I do not believe I am alone in this behaviour. A book entitled *Creationism; the truth* is certainly not likely to be bought by many evolutionists, just as one entitled *Evolution; the facts of life* is unlikely to be read by many creationists. The same applies in real life. Fans of two opposing football teams do not tend to sit together in the stadium. Not if they have any sense. Nor do many hugely obese people date anorexics.

We are inextricably drawn to those who are like us. Or rather, we are drawn to those who share our views and are, therefore, more likely to like us. We are prepared to learn and expand our horizons, as long as we do not have to change our essential vantage point. I, for example, am an Arsenal fan and always will be. Over time, my feelings and the way I support my team may change, but I will not change my team.

With this book, I certainly do not pretend to change or challenge anyone's beliefs, alliances or behaviour. I simply propose a perspective on existing ones that promotes empathy and understanding by focusing on the common underlying fears and desires that inspire our beliefs and behaviour. I would like to think that the final title for the book, *The Art of Being Human,* reflects the humanness of this perspective. To be honest, though, I plumped for the new title because it is shorter, quirkier, easier to remember and less likely to alienate readers from cultures where therapy is an alien concept for many.

The challenge of appealing to readers with conflicting points of view is not a new one for me. With my first book, *Safe Space*, I endeavoured to bolster the bridge between the worlds of hypnotherapy and psychotherapy by combining a therapeutic model specific to anxiety with techniques and procedures from the worlds of hypnotherapy, counselling and neuro-linguistic programming.

This book also pretends to act as a bridge, but rather than try to find a common ground for professionals from within different fields it does so for people with different world views, football teams, dreams and obsessions.

It would be easy to assume that writing such a book requires a meticulous sifting of the personal in order to isolate the impersonal. This book, however, is far from being the fruit of longs hours of academic investigation. It is more an expression of my own

A Personal View

personal journey in search of belonging and intimacy - two *essentials of being* I felt I had not fully experienced, partly because of the circumstances imposed upon me as a child and partly out of the life choices I made as an adult to compensate for my lack: I was born in a country I have never revisited. I am the product of a broken home. I have loved and lost. I have been expelled from two countries and presently live in four. For long periods of my life I spoke a language that was not my mother tongue. I am married to someone whose religion and culture I do not share and have a child with two nationalities and who, culturally, is both Christian and Muslim. I have buried both my mother and my father. I am currently sailing through mid-life and, ever since I can remember, I have felt that something has been hidden from me - a memory, truth or secret. This something I have glimpsed in dreams and I have spent my whole life trying to uncover. At this point in my life, I believe this hidden piece will remain forever hidden because it has been forged out of my fear of dying and my desire to be immortal - the subject of this book.

Such circumstances may seem exaggerated and difficult to empathise with. My own view is that they are merely variations of most people's experience.

After all, who among us still lives in the place they were born? Who cannot identify a rupture in their family? Who has never felt uprooted or homesick? Who has not been ravaged by love and loss? Who has not felt they were speaking a different language in their own home? Who does not live in a multicultural world? Who does not feel the internal conflict of a fragmented self? Who does not yearn to retrieve something lost? Who is not getting older? Who does not sense they are hiding something from themselves? Who has not dreamed of death?

Although it is my personal experience that stoked my desire to write this book, as a professional I have tried to be congruent with the thinking of the time, especially in the fields of psychology and science. Two therapists presently providing the general public with insight and understanding about the mind and the emotions are the existential psychotherapist Irvin Yalom and the psychologist John Rowan. From the world of science, the evolutionist Richard Dawkins has also provided a wealth of accessible information about the human species and how it has evolved.

I do not wish to compare this book with those of such eminent professionals, nor do I share all their views. This book is certainly not as therapeutic or brave as Yalom's determined look at death in *Staring at the Sun*. It is not as psychologically informative as John Rowan's theories on subpersonality in *Discover Your Subpersonalities*. The views expressed in this book do not carry the same weight as Dawkins' science in *The Selfish Gene*. Nor am I as certain in my views as Dawkins is in *The God Delusion*. I certainly do not share his conviction that God is a delusion because I am not privy to enough information about life, the universe and everything to make such a claim. I do, however, share Dawkins' willingness to express possibilities that not everyone is comfortable about hearing. With Yalom I share the view that by avoiding the subject of death we close many doors to happiness and fulfilment. With John Rowan I share his conclusion about our chances of finding wholeness and internal peace when he says, "There never comes a time when we can abandon our multiplicity and lay down in a perfect and final unity." Like Rowan, I believe that the best we can do is to find ways of making the quest to feel whole less violent and destructive while maintaining our own individual angles, colours and quirks.

I would like to think that my own modest grain of sand, rather than revealing anything new, is to have expressed as simply and in as digestible a way as the subject permits, what the reader already knows and suspects - that at some deep level we are haunted and inspired by our own demise more than we would like to believe.

Such a view is not one I would advise anyone to contemplate for long. It is far too detached to linger on and serves no real purpose, other than as a catalyst for self-awareness, empathy and understanding. This book is certainly not the basis for therapy, nor does it pretend to offer an independent big-picture world view. For these reasons, I have kept the book quirky, to dip in and out of, so that the reader, as soon as possible, can get on with practising the art of being human.

John Hayes was born in Malawi of British parents and is a member of a multicultural family that flits between two continents and three languages. He has a therapeutic practice in Winchester, lectures widely and is author of *Safe Space*, a critically acclaimed manual for treating anxiety and panic.

www.johnhayesuk.com

JOHN HAYES

Safe Space

A self-help manual & therapist's guide for treating anxiety and panic
ISBN: 978-0-9558071-0-7
£8.95

For therapists dealing with trauma-related anxiety and anyone seeking to understand and overcome their own, *Safe Space* offers a long-term solution by combining a therapeutic model specific to anxiety with a step-by-step procedure that draws from the worlds of hypnotherapy, counselling and neuro-linguistic programming.

The book includes a comprehensive explanation of the theory behind the procedure and a practical introduction to hypnosis and self-hypnosis. To aid comprehension, the book is interlaced with a compassionate and inspiring case history.

No knowledge or previous experience of hypnosis is required to benefit from this book.

"This book stands in a class of its own. The *Procedure* and *Tools for Change* section are second to none."
The Hypnotherapist

"Insightful, creative and psychologically informed."
MBACP Counsellor and Supervisor

"A mini-classic."
Hypnotherapy Articles

"A wonderful example of a clearly passionate and knowledgeable practitioner in action."
The Hypnotherapy Journal